NORF

Brereton

Propect Press
Native Guides

Norfolk Tales

By B.Knyvet Wilson

Introduced by Sir Timothy Colman K.G.

With a Foreword by the late Mr Russell Colman

Illustrated by David Jones

Prospect Press
Native Guides

Native Guides Dialect Series
Editor George Nobbs

Norfolk Tales
First published as *Norfolk Tales and Memories* in 1930
and
More Norfolk Tales in 1931
By B.Knyvet Wilson
First published by Jarrold and Sons, Limited.

*This new edition completely revised and edited by George Nobbs
with illustrations by David Jones, published Easter 2005*

ISBN
0-9545521-4-8

Printed in England by
Page Brothers, Norwich

Publisher's Note

In 1930 Mr Brereton Knyvet Wilson, a well-liked and much-respected local solicitor, published a small collection of Norfolk stories. He did so with but one idea, as he said in his introduction – *'that these Norfolk anecdotes may be preserved in print'*. So great was the response to his efforts that within a year, he was obliged to publish a second collection which appeared in 1931. He did so because, as he pointed out, *'a great many people have informed me that I have omitted most of the best yarns!'* Although the first volume contained some personal reminiscences, when it came to the stories themselves, Mr Knyvet Wilson never claimed to have written them. As he, with characteristic modesty, admitted *'I am not of course the author of them. I am simply a collector or editor.'*

Many of his contributors are listed in the second collection as *'some of the best known protagonists of our Norfolk wit, humour and phraseology'* – Miss M.M. Raven, of Yoxford; Canon Marcon, of Edgefield; Mr G. W.Stebbings, of Norwich; Mr Guy G. Sooby, of Swaffham; Mr Roland Wilson, of Acle ; Mr J.A. Christie M.P. (the last two being his brother and brother-in-law respectively). He gave a special mention to Mr Bertram Steward –' *one of the most amusing raconteurs of the Norfolk story'* – who contributed a *'good many'* to the collection. He also thanked many others who remained anonymous.

One who was not listed as a contributor was none-the-less freely acknowledged in the text - *'Mr Russell Colman has, as every one knows, a fine assortment of Norfolk stories. One or two of them I am tempted to repeat, with his permission.'* In fact it was more than one or two. Russell Colman as long serving Chairman of Norfolk County Council, Lord Lieutenant of the counties of Norfolk and Norwich, High Steward of Great Yarmouth, local magistrate and head of the Colman's Mustard Empire was *the* authority on Norfolk stories and his name appears on the title page of the first collection as the author of the Foreword which appears below.

Brereton Knyvet Wilson came from a long line of distinguished Norfolk figures. His obituary in the *E.D.P.* described him as a man of many parts whose *'tall and thickly built form gave him more the appearance of a country squire than a lawyer'* .He was a famous local cricketer as well as a gifted singer and musician. His family was originally from

Ashwellthorpe and claimed kinship with the barony of Berners and his uncle Sir Arthur Knyvet Wilson had become First Sea Lord in 1910. He practiced law in Norwich until, (despite being in his late 40s) he volunteered for the Forces during the First World War, taking it also as an appropriate time to retire from his law practice. After the War he spent his remaining years at Cringleford.

Of the two volumes published in 1930 and 1931 a certain amount of material has been omitted. The original title was *Norfolk Tales and Memories* and it is the personal memories of Mr Brereton Knyvet Wilson and stories of his parents, brothers and their servants that have been largely omitted although a certain amount has been retained to give a flavour of the original. But it is the Tales themselves that have been given pride of place in this new collection. Although not the author of them, Brereton Knyvet Wilson greatly deserves our thanks for collecting and recording these stories for future generations to enjoy again. In this new edition some of the more obscure have been left out, and some have needed to be shortened or slightly re-phrased for the sake of clarity, but in all essentials this is a distillation of the greatest of the classic Norfolk Tales.

The original two collections had very few photographs and only one drawing and that was a cartoon by Brigadier General Green that appeared in the second volume. This new volume is illustrated by local artist David Jones who shows a rare gift of portraying Norfolk and its' people as it, and they, appeared in the author's day.

Finally I would like to thank Sir Timothy Colman K.G. for agreeing to add his introduction to complement the Foreword that his grandfather first wrote some 75 years ago.

As Mr Knyvet Wilson himself said '*Perhaps a hundred years hence, if there should be a copy remaining of this little book which has not been burnt for its vulgarity will some Norfolk man then say (in the best Oxford accent) 'I cannot really imagine that our rude forefathers ever pronounced the beautiful English language in such a blatantly ridiculous style and fashion. The ancient who promulgated this ridiculous work was drawing on his very inadequate imagination!' Well, 'Drat him! I say, and let's get on with it.'*

George Nobbs   Native Guides Ltd

Introduction by Sir Timothy Colman K.G.

When Mr Knyvet Wilson's 'Norfolk Tales' were first published in 1930 Russell Colman, my grandfather, was invited to write a foreword.

He deeply loved everything about Norfolk, the County in which he was born and lived his life. I can well remember as a young boy sitting at his table and chuckling at his seemingly limitless fund of Norfolk stories. They had and still have a blend of inimitable charm, logic, brevity and simple wit. Norfolk today is changing fast, and the use of its own special dialect, so difficult to record in writing, will inevitably vanish with time.

These Norfolk Tales reflect a bygone age when rural life, which most of these stories reflect, was for certain a hard existence. Humour had to be home made. What is remarkable and gratifying today however, is how much is now being done to preserve our memories and knowledge of the Norfolk dialect.

Our thanks are due to many. No list can be complete but the Norfolk Poet John Kett, Colin Riches, Eric Fowler (Jonathan Mardle), Sidney Grapes (Boy John), and Lilias Rider Haggard must surely be included as also Keith Skipper and those behind the recent launch of Friends of the Norfolk Dialect (FOND).   The Sound Archive at the new Norfolk Archive Centre is making an invaluable contribution preserving on tape what my grandfather used to proudly call "the vernacular".

I commend these stories, and many others for the enjoyment of all who love the County and its special humour, and I wish every success to this new edition of 'Norfolk Tales'.

Timothy Colman

There follows the Foreword that Sir Timothy's grandfather Mr Russell Colman, long-serving Chairman of Norfolk County Council and an equally popular Lord Lieutenant, wrote for the first edition in 1930.

FOREWORD

It has fallen to my lot to take on more than a few jobs which I was very inadequately fitted to carry out. Whether, in the slang of to-day, I have succeeded 'in getting away with it' is not for me to say.

In the present case I have been invited to write a Foreword to a book of Norfolk stories. It happens that I love stories, and I delight in Norfolk, both the county and its dialect, but how, and what, to write is the puzzle.

I should not attempt this task were it not for the fact that I welcome any effort made to preserve my 'Native'. My fear is that it is bound to disappear, and at no distant date. Until the outbreak of the Great War Norfolk was an isolated, or outlying, portion of Great Britain; but as the result of that event, so many speakers of English and other strange languages became resident in our midst, and so many Norfolk men of a young and impressionable age were thrown together for long periods with those who spoke a strange tongue, that it is not to be wondered at if contamination resulted.

To take but one instance: I can remember the time when, in the country districts of Norfolk, to hear an 'h' mispronounced was a cause of astonishment, though as much could not be said within the confines of the city.

To-day, alas! the fault has 'caught on', and who is to arrest its travel ? This I regard as nothing less than a disaster. If we can't have 'Norfolk', at least let us have 'English'. Well do I remember the following instructions called down the rink during a curling match by an individual whose aspirates had not received the attention they merited. He desired that Mr. Brown should place his curling-stone with some nicety on a particular spot, in order to guard - but not to promote - another stone. Putting his broom down to indicate the spot, he gave these instructions: 'Ere's where I want you, Mr. Brown; *right 'ere. Whatever you* do, don't be 'ard ; I'd rather 'ave you *'ogged* than *'eavy* this time.' That's English as it is sometimes spoken, but it was never so spoken in Norfolk, and my hope is that it never will be.

I have never experienced any difficulty in *speakin* ' Norfolk', but - quite frankly - I do not know how to write it. If I have not forgotten my schoolboy lessons there are five vowels, and sometimes two extra. For 'Norfolk' that does not appear to me to be anything like what I require.

Take the following sentence and render it into 'Norfolk': 'There's nothing ever goes down that old driftway, unless it be a farm-cart'

'There's *northen* ever go down that *ood* driftway *doo* that's only a *farm-cart'*. Now, in all the five words I have italicized I want a fresh supply of vowels, and unless I may have them I can't write 'Norfolk'.

This being the position, all that remains for me to do is to stop writing the Foreword, and this I will do; but just let me tell you the following, and those who can speak 'Norfolk' will be able to make good my shortcomings.

A Norfolk man, long absent, returned to the county hungering for a sound of the language he had never forgotten. He took a stroll down a lane, and presently detected the presence of some labourers at work on the other side of the fence.

He paused to listen to their conversation. This is what he heard:

'He saay t'me, he saay, " *Whatever aar* yew a do'en' with that there muck?"

" Do'en' with that there muck!" I saay. " Aarn't I a loden on it," I saay, "on t'r this here caart ?"

" Caart !" he saay. " Wor aar yew a go'en' t'r dew with it," he saay, " when your ha' loded it ?"

" Dew with it!" I saay. " Aarn't I a go'en' to caart it inter the garden and spreed it ?" I saay.

" Spreed it" he say. "I'll *spreed* you!" '

Norfolk stories in print seem, to a Norfolk eye at any rate, somewhat cold. The ear clamours for the warmth of intonation and of accents which are so necessarily the very essence of dialect.

I have written my Foreword and find I have not so much as mentioned the author or his book. This just confirms the truth of my opening sentence.

I do congratulate Mr. Knyvet Wilson on his pluck in tackling such a job as trying to put 'Norfolk' into print. It is not to be expected that a 'foreigner' will be able to make much of the stories he has collected, but there are so many of us who have the good fortune to call Norfolk our home that we at any rate shall regard ourselves as everlastingly in his debt.

RUSSELL J. COLMAN

PROLOGUE

As a general rule, the man or woman who decides to unload the small happenings of his or her career upon the public fails to interest and merely succeeds in wearying the patient reader.

In this little effort there will, at least, be very little of the Ego - nothing that can be avoided. Let me at once plead with my readers for a clear understanding. Most of my life has been lived in Norfolk, in which county my family has lived for very many hundreds of years. I deeply love the county and its people, and the small stories and happenings told in this little book are told in all kindness, and with but one idea, i.e. that some of these Norfolk anecdotes may be preserved in *print*. I do not think I know of any similar work. This is due partly to the well-known difficulty of expressing the Norfolk dialect in the written word. Of course it is quite impossible to give the 'lilt' of the language. The Norfolk man begins his sentence - if it be a question - very low down in the scale, and ends it a full octave or more above his original pitch.

For the last fifty years or more I have (with only a few years absence) been soaked in Norfolk ways, speech, humour, customs, and superstitions. From my late father (who was a Norfolk rector for 50 years) I have heard hundreds of stories which have at all events appealed to my sense of humour. Let me again repeat that in no case would I willingly offend any of my old country friends. I have too deep a love for them, their conversation, and their ways.

I am delighted to hear that these little Norfolk stories have been so much appreciated by people who have left the county for 'foreign parts', or who are compelled - poor mortals - to live outside the old county. So the object of this little book is to put on record a few Norfolk stories, a few quaint phrases, and to chronicle a few memories of the past fifty years.

I apologise to many friends to whom most of these stories may be chestnuts. I am not of course the *author* of them. Therefore I am simply a collector or editor. Now collector has an unpleasant sound, suggesting rates or taxes. There have been hundreds of editors. I have therefore decided to call myself a *redactor*. No one (outside a crossword puzzle) has ever before been a *redactor*. In this capacity I have gone very carefully through these little yarns, and am able to issue the usual certificate, *edited and found correct.*

B. Knyvet Wilson

What one doan't think of, another dew. (see page 20)

Great are the Norfolk man's powers of invention as to actual words, sentences, and meanings. One could write at great length on this fascinating facility of his, but I can only mention a very few. That inimitable raconteur and authority on Norfolk stories, Mr. Fitch (present Rector of Sheringham), has mentioned many in his very enjoyable lectures on the subject. I did not, however, hear him refer to the following expressions.

'No, sir, I didn't *imitate* to hit him.' This word hardly means *pretend* as I understand it, still less copy, but it means *start.* Then, of course, there is the amazing transformation of the 'o' in Norfolk. My wife went into a well-known grocer's shop in Norwich and asked for some *soap.* The young man brought her some packets of Symington's, or somebody else's, desiccated soup. She explained that she wanted *soap* 'to wash with'. ' Oh,' he said, 'I see, you want *soup*'! - and brought her soap!

Then I love the manufactured past tense. Any Norfolk gardener will tell you, 'Yes, sir, I *mew* that grass yesterday,' or 'That there old path was *hand-wed* only last Tuesday.' Then, when small plants are set in irregular lines, they 'mock' - a very curious use of the word. When things are on the slant, they are 'on the sosh', or on the 'skute'. One old gardener of my father's described the 'corbie steps' on Hedenham Hall as being 'all snotchy-like' - a most eloquent description.

I believe that the abbreviation 'bor' (for neighbour) is dying out. It was certainly in more common use in my young days than it is now. I like to hear a man say, 'He come up to *mine* last night,' and 'yours' is, I think, used in the converse manner. A 'dow' for a woodpigeon, is, of course, a corruption of 'dove'. Hinges are 'jimmers' and 'tittamatauta' (I don't know if it is spelt right) is a 'see-saw'. The word 'doubt', too, is used in a curious way. 'I *doubt* he oon't goo,' means, really, 'I'm quite sure he won't go.' There is practically no element of doubt whatever in the speaker's mind.

The word 'hull' is of course Norfolk for 'hurl'. The late Bob Lake, that excellent character from Brancaster, amused the Prince of Wales (the future King Edward VIII, Duke of Windsor) highly when playing golf against him at Brancaster.

'Now then,' said the Prince,'shall we toss for honour?'

'Goo on, sir,' said Bob, 'hull it up!'

Hull is a much stronger word than 'cop'. I cannot think what the origin of cop is. It merely expresses a gentle throwing, a 'lobbing', so to speak. 'Cop us over that therem, 'bacca, Tom,' is an instance.

'Gay', as a rule, means 'spotted'. A good woman in our parish was quite proud of her boy, who had developed a very strong lot of measles. 'My boy,' she said, 'he's as gay as a leopard.'

The word 'wrought' is interesting. It is an old-fashioned word, and one of its synonyms is 'laboured', though one is more accustomed to its use in a 'skilled labour' sense, such as in 'wrought iron', and in connection with the delicate work of gold and silversmiths. But in Norfolk one hears,

'Afore I coom hare I wrought on yin side o' Swaffham.'

Of course a Norfolk man's donkey is his 'dicka', and his big toes are his 'gret tom toes' - why, I do not know. The use of negatives is very curious. When I used to ask our old postman if there were any letters, he would answer,

He's as gay as a leopard (see page 13)

'No, sir, there ain't not none not for nobody!' If two negatives make an affirmative there really ought to have been some letters for there were six distinct negatives in this sentence!

'Up at Harwich' is a quite well-known expression for a state of general confusion. That this is a relic of the past seems to be certain, and refers to the turmoil created by William, Prince of Orange, when he landed at Harwich

THE PHRASEOLOGY OF NORFOLK

This is a fascinating subject and comprises a great many subtle mouldings of the English language into strange and ingenious phrases, but frequently takes into use coined words which, euphoniously at any rate, express their meaning very cleverly indeed. Since my previous effort I have remembered and come across many more examples worth recording, and even now, doubtless, am only on the fringe of the subject. Such words as 'dodman' (snail), 'fleet' (shallow), 'mavish' (thrush), 'bloodolpher' (bullfinch) are illustrations. Then the words 'gain', 'ongain', and 'more gainer', meaning easy or willing, difficult or unwilling, and still more difficult and obstinate, are in very common use.

I love the expression 'He live *upright'*. In my ignorance I used to think that this meant that the person designated lived an upright and pious life. Not at all. He is respected and looked up to because he has no need to *stoop* and scratch the ground for a living; in other words, he is independent.

Last year I was trying to find a way to a 'shoot' in the country and asked a labourer the way to the house. He shaded his eyes with one hand and said, 'Well, now, yer see *them* linen hangin' out there?' No doubt the plural is, in a sense, correct, but it is unusual.

Some of my friends pronounce ordinary English words in a quaint way. They make a 'sturt' instead of a 'start'. Various diseases have very quaint synonyms. One old man had 'multiplication of the bowels'; another had 'haricot veins'; a third had 'bellicose veins'; an old woman had 'information and ammonia'; and still another had 'kangarene of the fut' - a lively sort of complaint, one would imagine.

My brother's old yardman, Henry (hero of several stories), was found one day sniffing round the kitchen, where a hare was being cooked. The housekeeper asked him what he wanted. He passed his hand over his mouth, gave her a beseeching look, and remarked, 'I doan't know as ever I taasted *juggled* hare !' Henry also said that he and his missus only took in the daily paper when there was a 'good marder'; 'we likes a good marder, we does,' he concluded. Henry had a daughter who developed certain twitchings of the face and limbs, and he took her to his doctor; on my brother inquiring what the doctor had said, old Henry said, 'Well, I can't rightly recollect what that was he said. Ah ! yes, I know what that was - that was the *wiper's dance*.' He also was very pleased with '*all them red 'excursions*' growing all round my brother's house.

My friend, the late Mr. Gerard F. Blake, used to be very much amused when he recalled a certain clerk of one of our Norwich courts who on one occasion opened the proceedings of the court with 'Brooks agin Barnard. Barnard hare?' An old Norfolk farmer given a ride in a springless farm-cart over a bumpy lane in the frost remarked, 'Dang me if that worn't enow to *jatter* yer teeth out!' Only a few days ago I inquired, from a fine old Norfolk gardener, how his master (an invalid) was getting on. 'Well, sir, pretty middlin' said the old man; 'he keep on *jammin'* about!' Very expressive.

STRANGE NORFOLK EXPRESSIONS

A land-agent I know was arranging for the drainage of some lands. One of the fields was an awkward shape and ran downhill to a point. The agent asked the bailiff how he would propose to drain that field. The latter gesticulated freely and said, 'Well, yew'd hev one old drain come *soshin* and t'other *yin!*' - and this can only be understood by a real Norfolker. Then the much-used word 'hain', meaning 'raise'. 'Nasen' for 'nests', is also queer.

A conversation heard between two labourers is very instructive. 'Whare are yew a-goin' to, Billa ?'

'I ain't a-goin' nowheres, George; I'm now a-comin' back!'

Then the old Norfolk word 'mardle' is very apt, and means, of course, a long-drawn-out gossip.

An angry mother will always threaten to 'sort' her child - probably with a stick; or she may 'right-side' him.

On one of the Norwich motor-parks the other day I remarked to the attendant that the cars were rather carelessly parked. He said, 'Yes, sir ; people fare wunnerful *cattankerous* to-day. I can't do nothin' with'em.'

'Clever' does not convey the same meaning exactly to the Norfolk man as it conveys to the outer world. He distrusts a 'clever' man, and reads *clever* as deep and cunning. My brother-in-law Mr. J. A. Christie, who was then M.P. for South Norfolk was talking to an old farmer (a supporter) just at the time when he was being opposed by a Labour candidate. Mr. Christie - quite honestly - said, 'I'm told, that my opponent is a very clever man'; to which the reply came, 'Lord love you, Sir! *We* don't want a *claver* man for South Norfolk! We want *you*.' Happily Mr. Christie knew that no 'backhander' was intended.

The word 'several' (or 'saveral' in Norfolk) is very curiously used. In ordinary parlance, of course, the word expresses up to four, five, or six persons or things, or (as the dictionary has it) 'a few separately or

a sort stick (see opposite)

individually'. But in Norfolk we mean a crowd. So a man describing the crowd at a 'needle' football match at the 'Nest' would say, 'Oh, yes, there was *saveral* people there!' In addition to these curious expressions I have already quoted, Canon Marcon mentions the following:

On the 'sosh' or 'soish', or on the 'scute' or 'skute', means on the slant, not straight; 'spolt',describes wood in its sapless winter state; 'kedgy', agile for his years ; 'sunket', a hash or made dish - not honest beef, mutton, or pork; 'frolic', a good old-fashioned word for 'outing' or entertainment.

Then a 'shy girl' is anything *but shy;* to 'knab' (or nab) the rust, to take offence (origin unknown); 'do' and 'don't' for 'if ' or 'otherwise'; 'summerly' for 'summer ley' ; 'olland' - i.e. the old land, grass land at its last - at its *first* it is 'new ley' ; 'cuts' and 'gays' are printed and coloured pictures respectively; to 'acknowledge me suffun' is to bestow a gift upon the speaker ; 'clung', not quite dry.

A 'jolly' man is one inclined to obesity; 'fierce', spoken of a wound which looks red and inflamed; 'lug' the ear; to 'crowd' is to push; 'no matters' not very well ('I doan't fare no matters to-day'); and 'together', that well-known term when addressing several persons, as in 'Now then together, less we be a-goin'.'

Of coined words Canon Marcon mentions 'tilly-willy', of small, fiddling things, such as the drawing out of small onion-shoots from the ground; and of a sick person's tied-up head 'that dew fare to shoot an' *bulk* an' stab and dart like anything'. Then a 'frail' is a basket and coarse cloth is a 'dwile'.

An old Norfolk expression is 'Thass afore your mother bought a shovel' meaning apparently that the matter being referred to is above the head or beyond the comprehension of the person being addressed.

NEGATIVES

I have already mentioned this subject in relation to our old postman but Canon Marcon is also very instructive on the use of negatives by the Norfolk man, and asks why this should be such a habit of his. He shies at an affirmative or a positive as something to be avoided. The advice given to one called as a witness before the magistrates was, 'Never you know nothin'; nobody carn't never get over that'. A bricklayer was testing a wall with his plumb-line, which of course had to be quite accurate. His verdict was, 'There, that ain't far wrong.'

Canon Marcon said, 'Why on earth can't you say it's *quite all right*?' He looked surprised and said, 'Well thass our way, I s'pose.' And another man admiring a new selfbinding machine in the harvest-field said, 'The man what put that thing together worn't no fule' - not that the man was a clever man or that it was a clever invention. When a good man has died the comment on him is 'He'll be missing' which

that dew fare to shoot an'bulk an'stab an' dart (see opposite)

stands for great praise, and the Canon sums up, 'It is to these inadequate expressions that the listener has to supply the fuller meaning.

The explanation is, perhaps, that it is an extreme form of caution, generated by the instinct of self preservation, and 'non-committalism'; an extreme form of it is silence, with perhaps laconic monosyllables.

But silence has its advantages; you can the better pick your neighbour's brains if you say nothing.'

Then watch two Norfolk labourers studying some new machine or other invention they have never seen before. It's a 'guinea to a hayseed' that one will say, 'Lawk! how they do get these hare things up,' and the other will say, 'Ah! what one doan't think of another dew!'

the prize goat (see opposite)

THE PRIZE GOAT

A certain Norfolk man laid out sixpence in a raffle at the local horticultural show. To his great gratification he won first prize - a goat.

He led it home in triumph. The same evening several of his friends paid him a visit of congratulation. 'They tell me yew ha' done well, George,' said one 'Yew ha' won an owd goot, ha'en't ye?'

' Ah! I hev an all,' said George; ' and thass a good goot, that is."

' Come on then, George, less we hev a look at 'um.' But George was very mysterious. 'He's all right, I ha' gor'um'.

' Well, where is he?' said John.

' Well, thass like this hare,' said George: ' there ha' bin a lot o' these owd tarkey thieves about o' late and I hev a mind to keep my owd goot, so I ha' put him away safe'

' Well, then, where ha' ye put 'um? ' said John.

' I ha' gor'um in the Missis' and my bedroom,' said George.

'Coo! my heart alive! George' said John. 'What about the smell?'

'Well there, John,' said George, ' *th' owd goot doan't fare to mind that a mite!'*

HENRY AND THE PIGS

My brother had a yardman called Henry who was a great character. He had a high opinion of his own mental ability and was forever keen to explain the phenomena of nature to those who knew much more about the matter than he did. On these occasions he would wear a cunning smile and assume a confidential manner. Once my brother was watching him fill the pigs' 'trows' with liquid food, and twelve piglets were greedily snapping, biting, and squealing to get at it. Old Henry looked at my brother, assumed his usual grin, and said, ' Ah! he was no fule as fust called them pigs; *thas just what they are - PIGS!'*

HENRY GIVES ADVICE

Henry was also very keen on what he called a 'bit of sput' (there is no other way of spelling the word 'sport' in the Norfolk dialect, and it rhymes with 'foot'). He loved going out 'brushing' with the 'guns', but his exceedingly loud and outspoken comments on their abilities were apt to get him into trouble. Did a cock pheasant nearly knock the hat off one of the 'guns' so that the killing of it was almost an unavoidable necessity, he would shout:

Thas just what they are – PIGS! (see overleaf)

'Brayvo, sir! Brayvo ! I thowt you'd get him. Thass capital, that is; yew ha' done well!'

On the other hand, when a certain Colonel J-, a fine shot with a somewhat irascible nature, happened to snap at a rabbit and missed it, old Henry was very indignant.

'Oh, dare! Oh, dare! thass bad, that is. Thass no good, sir, he's gone! I see yer shot goo, sir; half a yard behind him you was. Petty, sir, petty! *Nice raabit* he was too!' The Colonel was so indignant that old Henry had to be sent home.

He was also full of suggestions. He suggested to my brother that he should put a large tub on each side of his front door and plant them 'with them there hy-geraniums' (hydrangeas).

OLD CHARLEY

Several parish clerks, I remember, in my young days gave me great joy. I don't know if the practice of the reading of the Psalms in alternate verses is still carried on. The clerk at Fritton had his own pew and large ancient prayer-book. This book had the names of many kings and queens crossed out and filled in with the names of their successors. Old Charley, our parish clerk for many years, was a bit of a celebrity. My father would read one verse, and the congregation and old Charley would take the next. But Charley was not to be hurried, and the congregation invariably finished their reading while Charley was still in the air. To us boys this was a pure delight, especially when old Charley rendered 'Unto him appeared the Lord in Zion in perfect beauty' as 'Unto him appared the Lord in Zion, - *a* puffick *bewty* !'

Also he had never heard of the word 'equity' and obviously thought it a misprint, so 'His word shall be done in truth and equity' was always rendered as 'His wad shall be done in truth and *iniquity*'. Hardly the same thing!

Once when my father was preaching his Harvest Festival sermon and the church (including the gallery at the west end - since taken down) was packed, there was an ominous crack from one of the posts of the gallery. My poor father was somewhat 'put off his stroke' by old Charley's loud voice addressed to the alarmed people in the gallery, 'Dew yew know you're all a-comin' down there!'

It was afterwards said that a parson from an adjacent village, kindly helping us with his voice in the choir in the gallery, beat all records in getting down the steps into the belfry.

THE DECOY

Rumour also had it that old Charley was the hero of the tale of another Harvest Thanksgiving at which a neighbouring parson was taking duty for my father. Old Charley, as usual, carried round the collecting plate.

the decoy

When the service was over this parson, with a shocked and grieved face, confronted old Charley in the vestry.

'I am terribly grieved, Charley' he said, 'to have to state that I distinctly saw you abstract a coin from the collection.'

Old Charley, who was as honest as the day was long, chuckled.

'Lord luv you, sir,' he said, ' thass my old *decoy*. I ha' put him in to start 'em off for nigh on twenty years, and so o'course he's got to come out agin !'

A SPLENDID EXAMPLE

My father was once taking an old gentleman in the parish, to task for failure to attend church. He had a son who was somewhat simple-minded. This son invariably turned up twice on Sunday and delighted in helping old Charley to ring the bells, etc. My father, somewhat unfortunately, said,

'Your son is a splendid example. He is most useful to us, comes to church regularly, rings the bells,' etc., to which the old gentleman replied,

'Ah! sir, I doubt he woont come if *he had got his proper know'* to which retort there did not seem to be much answer.

ONE GLASS O'MILD

Old John, another of our parish clerks, was also a local 'worthy'. Usually very steady, he had, very occasionally, a ' break-out'. At service one Sunday morning my dear mother noticed that John's face had been terribly through the wars, and was adorned in many places with strips of adhesive plaster. This could not be put down to clumsiness in shaving, for it was very obvious that John had not risked a shave that morning, so my father was duly notified, and poor old John was summoned to the vestry after service, confronted by my father and our fine old churchwarden, Tom Brown, and asked to account for the condition of his face at a Sunday morning service.

The old man was extraordinarily glib and plausible. 'Well, sir, ye know, sir, that was like this hare. Yew know, Mr. Brown, as I goes to my club in Henmal [Hempnall] every Saturday, sir? Well, sir, I went yesterday, and I had one glass o' mild bare - only one, sir, all day, sir. Well, sir, as I was a-comin' home, sir, just arter I got opposite yar midder, sir, near yar house, sir, and that was a-getting' wery dark, sir, there was a man layin' for me in the holl, and all of a sudden he up and struck me across the hid, sir, he did, and when I come to meself like, ye know, sir, there I was a-layin' in the holl, and them there old brumbles, they must a made these hare marks on my face.'

My easily beguiled father viewed the old man with sympathy, and was about to express it in words. Not so, however, old Tom Brown. He fixed old John with a hard and unbelieving eye, and issued his judgment in a deep voice. 'Goo on with ye, John, that was old *Bullard* hit ye!' And I'm afraid it was so *.

I heard of another old man, who was unaccustomed to anything stronger than mild ale. Some gentleman gave him a pint of ' Stingo', or some other very strong beer. Describing the result to his friends afterwards, he joyously remarked,

'Well, there!   I tell ye the tanpike worn't wide enough to hould me, noo, nor yit Mulbarton Common nayther !'

Bullards were one of the four Norwich Breweries which, together with Lacons of Yarmouth, supplied Norfolk with beer.

SUPERSTITIONS AND FANCIES

DO not think Norfolk folk are as superstitious as those in some other counties. In Essex, for example, I believe the superstitions of the people are amazing, and witchcraft is still strongly credited. But in many small ways the folk of our county have their strange beliefs, and who shall say whether or not they are justified in them? Take the matter of bees, for example.

Bees are uncanny things and must be humoured. A great many bee-keepers tell all their family secrets to the bees. My father was a most enthusiastic lover of these insects, whilst they and I were never without a disagreement, in which I, almost invariably, came off second best. I would respectfully take my father to task for his superstition when I heard him murmuring to his bees. He would reply, 'Quite right, of course, my boy, but it can't do any harm just to tell them what's going on in the family!' Then, of course, if there is a death in the family, the hives have to be 'draped' with crape; otherwise the bees will leave you. I remember that in my early days we had a frail German governess, who, I am sorry to say, was taken ill and died in the house. Next morning the cook came to my mother and stated that our old gardener, wanted a 'bit o' *black* to drape the bees'. Thinking that this was a good chance of checking the superstition my mother went out to see him and stated that she was certainly not going to encourage the idea.

'Very well, mum' he said; 'you'll see they 'oon't stay with yer' Now it is a somewhat strange coincidence that during the next week *every bee took its departure.* Certainly the old gardener didn't take them, for he was just as much afraid of them as I was.

My father and his bees were very much attached to each other - in a manner quite different to their attachment to me! During the last weeks of his life - and when he lay prostrate after a preliminary stroke, at the end of November 1900 - I was wandering rather sadly about the garden when I was surprised to see many of his bees buzzing about, though it was a bitter, frosty morning. I went in and told him about this and he was very much surprised. He explained that some time back he had 'clayed' them in, in their hives, for that winter. I examined the hives and could find no outlet. A few days later he died.

The day of his funeral was, I remember, a still more frosty day. There was no sun, and no appearance of any bees during the morning. In the afternoon a few hours after the funeral, my mother asked me to go up to the churchyard, some half-mile from the Rectory, and see that the grave was filled in and in order. There were, of course, lots of flowers on the grave, but I was surprised to find clouds of bees there as well. The materialist will doubtless say that where there are flowers there will be bees. I have not noticed them in *December*, before or since, and I prefer to think that they were saying 'Goodbye' to their old friend and master.

I remember an old villager who asserted to his dying day that he had a living frog in his inside. He had, he said, swallowed it when he (and it) was young, in a glass of water, and that it had been 'in his innards ever since'. It was apparently a useful animal, as it acted as a barometer.

'Law, maaster, when thass a-goin' to rain you should hare him sing, he do fair holler'.

A SIGN

The following story may, I think, fairly come under the head of 'superstitions'. A Vicar that I knew used to visit an old bed-ridden woman parishioner regularly once a week and read to her. She set great store on these visits. Once, however, the rector was called suddenly to London, forgot about the old lady, and did not send an excuse. On his return he hurried to see her and found her full of lamentations. After making his peace with her, she became somewhat mysterious and said,

'Well, now, yew know, sir, I ha' got suffen to tell yer. Since yew was here last I ha' had a wision!'

'Dear me,' said the rector, 'and what did the vision consist of?'

'Well, sir, I was a-layin' hare last Toosday I think it were, a little butter than a quarter arter fower I think that would be - when all of a sudden the door opened, and in come my pore husbin'. Well, sir, o' course that worn't my pore husbin' really, 'cos he ha' bin dead this *thatty* year, but I thowt that was him. Well, sir, he come across the floor, and come up to my bed, and he stroke my hid twice, he did, and he knelt him down and said a bewtiful prayer, he did, and then out he went. Now, sir, I can''t help thinkin' thass a sign, thass a *token,* that is!'

The rector was much impressed, and, lowering his voice to a reverential pitch, said, 'Well, of course, Mrs. G. these things are sometimes sent to warn us. Now what do you think it was a sign of ?'

'Well, sir, I can't help thinkin' - *thass a sign o' rain!'*

THEM OLD POLICEMEN

One day my father-in-law, the late Mr. James Christie, was passing his woodshed where a couple of his oldest estate men were working. He noticed a very choice bundle of billets carefully set aside. Later in the day he met old Henry going home with the bundle over his shoulder 'What have you got there, Henry?' he asked.

'Ah! thass just an old bundle of wood which noobody wouldn't never want', said Henry.

'Well, what do you think the policeman would do if he came along and found you with that wood?' To which old Henry replied, confidentially, 'Ah! sir, *them there old policemen will do anything!'*

This so amused my father-in-law that no more could be said.

THE EYE TEST

My late uncle, Dr. Tom Amyot, of Diss, told an amusing story of a patient of his, an old farmer who had developed cataract in both eyes.

My uncle decided to operate and did so. When the time arrived for the removal of the bandages the doctor was naturally anxious to know if the operation had been a real success. The blind was drawn up, and the old man exclaimed delightedly at seeing again ' th' ould cows and hosses', etc.

 After that my uncle tested his short sight with the family Bible. First he tried him with the small print of the text. The old man held it at various distances - near and far but exclaimed despondently, 'Noo, sir, thass no good!'

My uncle was very disappointed also, and tried him with the larger print such as 'The Acts'. Same result. Finally with the words ' Holy Bible' in letters half an inch high. There was a like result and a dead silence.

Then the old man said,' Happen thass 'cos I can't read, sir!'

POTTED RABBIT

Mr. Russell Colman has, as every one knows, a fine assortment of Norfolk stories. One or two of them I am tempted to repeat, with his permission. It appears that a Norfolk man came into a small legacy and at once bought a farm. This venture failed, and he took a small place in the neighbourhood of Thetford with the idea of making money out of the many rabbits there. He did fairly well at first, but his 'old woman' thought it was a bit too slow.

'You bring me in them raabits, George,' she said, 'and I'll deal with them.'

 George obeyed, and turned them into 'potted rabbit', and quite a little industry arose. Some time later one of his friends came to George and said,

'Ye know, George, I doan't fare to fancy that potted raabit of yours so much as I did. That doan't taste, nor yet that doan't smell as nice as that did. What do that mean?'

'Well, John,' said George, 'ye see them old raabits ain't so *frequent* as they used to be, and I has to put in a bit of hoss-meat just to spreed 'em out like.'

'Thass all right, George, but what sort of proportions do you put in ?'

'Oh, just fifta fifta,' said George.

'What do yew mean *fifta fifta* ?' asked his friend.

' Well,' said George, '*one hoss, one raabit!*'

MAKING THE WILL

Hare William, I'll tell Mr Brown what yew want ter say in yar will

A certain old farmer near Norwich lay a-dying of the *pewmonia* and *brownchitis*. In his later years he had married an extremely energetic second wife, much younger than himself. She, finding that her husband had neglected to make his will, began to be anxious as to her future. So she induced him to call in his lawyer, who came to take instructions. The old man made a very wheezy attempt at his 'instructions', so much so that his wife grew impatient.

'Hare, William,' she said, 'that ain't no manner o' good. Look hare, William, I'll tell Mr. Brown what yew want ter say in yar will - *jist you goo on with yer dyin' !*' (I don't think she really intended to be brutal.)

THAT OLD POOST MORTUM

An old man (call him Billa) who lived in a parish near Norwich was taken very ill and had to be removed to the hospital. There he had an operation, which unfortunately failed to save him, and he died. The hospital authorities telegraphed to his relatives asking permission to hold an autopsy on him to discover the exact cause of death. After some discussion and explanation the post mortem was held and the matter apparently ended. Some time later a friend of mine, living in the parish, was trying to persuade a woman to send her daughter (who was ill) to the hospital for treatment.

'Noo,' she said, 'I 'oon't hev her goo'

' Why ever not?' asked my friend.

'Why' she said, 'they mess and muck ye about at that there old horspital.' My friend assured her that she was mistaken, and that the hospital was noted for the kindness and attention of its doctors and nurses. The woman was still obstinate.

'Look at poor old Billa' she said. 'If he hadn't a had that old poost mortum *he'd a bin alive to this day!*'

A BAD JOB

My brother heard an amusing conversation at a corner of a street in a certain country village close to Norwich. Three men were standing there talking about a neighbour who had just been taken on as a drayman by Morgans Brewery and they looked very grave and serious. 'Poor old George!' said one, and sighed heavily.

'Ah, thass a bad job, that is,' said a second. (My brother imagined that poor George had lost his wife, suddenly, or maybe his favourite child).

'Yes, that that is' said the first. 'Look at all the bare he git, an' that doan't dew him a mite o' good. Pore feller, he ain't got noo *swaller.* What a waste!'

THE CONJURER

A Norwich professional conjurer attended a small village entertainment and was a great success. Later he went among the audience and produced marvellous things from their pockets. Presently he turned his attention to an old keeper, and said to the audience,

'Now, you will see, I shall have the pleasure of producing a live rabbit from this gentleman's left hand coat pocket', but was a little taken aback when the keeper replied,

'I doubt that'll be afore your time, maaster; I got an old ferret in there a'ready !'

THE COST OF TRAVELLING

Well do I remember dear old Mrs. Francis of our parish, who after threatening to become a centenarian unfortunately faded away in her hundredth year. For many years she had been bed-ridden, but a talk with her was most cheering, even to a somewhat impatient boy.

'Now, Master Knyvet,' she said to me once, 'how much do you think that I, in my long life, have spent on travellin'?' I couldn't possibly guess.

'Sixpence!' said the old dear. 'And that was because my husband took me up to Tombland Fair and lorst me, and I had to come home with the carrier!'

She had never seen a train. 'Nasty creepin', crawlin' things,' she called them. My father and I used to read to her. Once after a locum tenens, who had a very slight impediment in his speech, had visited her, she told my father that he was a nice man, but she didn't like his reading. ' He du *har and hukker so'*

THE HALF-MARRIED WOMAN

Another celebrity in our parish was known to the day of her death as the 'half-married woman'. This was because she had come to church to be married, and when the bridegroom had made all the necessary responses and my father had asked her the vital question 'Wilt thou have this man' etc., she had suddenly said,

'Noo! That I 'oon't,' and marched out of church, leaving my father and the groom staring at one another. She never made another venture, and was always thereafter known as the 'half-married woman'.

JEST A-STEPPING

One took a long time to grow old at Fritton. One old gentleman aged eighty-seven was discussing with my father the question of his son's future. His son's age was sixty-five.

'Ye see, sir,' he said, 'my son he's what you might call jest a-steppin' into manhood!'

I TOLD T' PARSON THAT WORNT A MITE O' USE

An archdeacon of Norfolk was inspecting the plate, furniture, and furnishings belonging to a church in an out-of-the-way village in Norfolk. On being taken round by the churchwarden, he was shocked to see that a great part of the churchyard had been ploughed up and sown down to wheat. So he said to the churchwarden,

'Mr. Brown, this is a terrible state of affairs! This won't do at all!'

'Ah! sir, you're right; I thowt you'd say that. I tould t' parson that there wheaten crop worn't a mite o' use. He'd a done a site better with a crop o' taters!'

he'd a done a site better with a crop o' taters

SHOOTING AND OTHER TALES

One old keeper I knew used, it was said, to be somewhat 'henpecked' at home. One day he went out with my brother, and they saw a curious sight. A hen pheasant had got its neck caught in the fork between two boughs and had hung itself. My brother turned to the keeper and said, 'Now what do you think of that?' The old man breathed very hard and then said 'Ah! now, sir, you'll notice that if anybody du anything fulish thass sure to be a *hin!*' I doubt if he ever told this story at home.

I heard of a party of rich Americans who took a shoot in Norfolk. On the first day out they announced very kindly beforehand that the bag would be sent to the Norfolk and Norwich Hospital at Norwich. Most of it was! It consisted of a rat, a female 'gun', and a beater. The rat was not sent!

Admiral Wilson of Swaffham, was very fond of a 'bit of sput'. An exceedingly eccentric parson, not far from Norwich, asked him to come over and shoot, and 'bring one or two more with you'. With great labour he collected three more 'guns', and after a long drive they all arrived at the Rectory, bright and early. Apparently too bright and early, for there was no sign of life whatever to be seen. After a lot of knocking and ringing, an upper window was raised and the parson appeared, his head adorned with a night-cap.

'What's this? What's this?' he asked, and, on being told, withdrew his head muttering,'Shoot! Bless my soul yes, shoot!' After a long wait the parson eventually appeared, and at once shouted for his gardening man. Ben came, and the parson said, 'Ben, seen the old hare about lately?'

'Noo,sir,' replied Ben, 'I ain't happened on her lately, I ain't.'

The party then, led by the parson, solemnly proceeded to the glebe meadow, in the middle of which was a small patch of scrub. The guns were carefully stationed round this scrub, whilst Ben went in and 'jammed' all over it with heavy boots. The 'old heer' was not at home, however - and that concluded the day's 'sput'.

THE WONDERS OF TELEGRAPHY

An amusing episode occurred at Forncett station. Employed there was a porter who was a bit of a wag. An old woman from our parish had a sudden summons to London to visit a daughter who was ill. She went off in a great 'flusteration', which continued to the time of her return to Forncett station some days later. As the cart which was to meet her was late, she was persuaded by the porter to take a seat in the waiting-room. When the cart did arrive and she had been safely stowed into it there was a sudden outcry. She had lost her umbrella - a friend of many years'

standing. Amid many wails she stated positively that she now remembered she had left it in *the London station* where she had had to wait. The
waggish porter had seen her with it in the waiting-room at Forncett, and
he at once went and discovered it there.

Instead of bringing it, however, he told her that if she would wait a few
minutes he would go and 'telegraph for it, and they would be sure to

If I hadn't a seen it with me own eyes I oont never hev believed it

send it'. He then dodged a few yards down the line, slipped up the iron
ladder of a telegraph post and *hung the umbrella on the wires.* He then
went to the old lady and insisted on her getting out of the cart.

'Thass all right, mum, we ha' telegraphed to London for your umbrella
and thass come down all right!' He then led her to a spot below the wires
and showed her the umbrella waving in the breeze. The old lady was
delighted.

'Well' she said, 'if I hadn't a seen it with me own eyes I oont never hev
believed it !'

HARVEST HOMES

The old *Harvest Home* seem, to a great extent, to be done away with. Well do I remember the great suppers, with songs and games. The supper was colossal, and such old-fashioned games as *Twilight*, a mysterious game connected with the spinning of a plate, were great fun. Popular too were such songs as *The Oak and the Ash* and the *Bonny Ivy Tree*, one (with about forty verses) all about a man and an oak tree:

> So this old man to Lunnon would goo
> To tell the King of all his woe,
> 'Twas all about fellin' an old oak tree
> And buildin' a house upon his own ground
> With a fol-de-rol-de-rol-de-rol-de-rol-de-rol-de-rido !

He goes to 'Lunnon' and sees the King, who gives him a shilling, but I never could quite gather the upshot of the whole story.

There was also a dear old gentleman who used to tell us, in a quavering voice, how fine it was 'to be a Varmer's Boy-hoy-hoy, to be a Varmer's Boy!'

One 'Farm Supper' at which I have the honour of being an annual guest is still a great affair. The 'carvings' are so many 'muscle grindings'; and, during this very serious business of eating and drinking, no time, breath or energy is wasted on conversation. In the opinion of us all there is a time for eating and another for conversation, and the one must not be allowed to interfere with the other. A steady 'champing' sound is unavoidable.

After supper comes the singing, washed down with quantities of mild beer. It is well known who will sing and who will not sing, but each must be asked. Generally it is 'Not to-night, sir, I'm afraid,' and, even when a certainty is called on, some difficulties have to be surmounted. His friends generally shout, 'Come on, Jimma!' and name the song they expect (possibly his whole repertoire), but 'Jimma' makes horrible noises in his throat, and says he has a 'cowld'. Also he says he can't remember the words, and has to be coaxed.

Eventually he shows signs of surrender, and his glass is refilled by his nearest neighbour. He takes a drink, rises, clears his throat once more and fixes his eyes on a distant beam of the room, so that no mundane affairs may fuddle his memory. And then he starts. Of course he doesn't want any 'accompaniment' - indeed, it would put him out altogether. The song may have anything from six to forty verses, and at the end of each verse it should have a refrain, which must not be encroached upon by the audience until it has been given by the singer alone. Then we all roar it together.

One very delightful effort is *The Dark-eyed Sailor*, which tells how a village maiden fell in love with young 'Will-i-yum', who went to sea and, in fact, became 'the dark-eyed sailor'. Before he leaves he breaks a sixpence, and they each treasure one half. The story is a little complicated, but I think 'Will-i-yum' is supposed to be drowned, and the maiden is consequently inconsolable for years. Just as she getting over it, and, I believe, thinking of getting married to some one else, a mysterious dark-eyed gentleman turns up in the village and, oddly enough, no one recognizes him at all until he produces his part of the broken sixpence, after which, of course, all turns out happily, and the song concludes, 'poetically', with

> *So, a cloudy mornin'*
> *Bring forth a parfect day,*

or words to that effect.

The tune has a sort of 'Gregorian' lilt, if such a thing be possible. When the song is finished the singer gives its title, *The Dark-eyed Sailor*, or whatever else it may be, sits down, and has his glass refilled. It is all very pleasant and enjoyable, and it does not at all matter if the same songs have been heard for many years past.

The courage of some of the young boys at these suppers is magnificent. If the lad can be induced to perform, he generally gets up, very red in the face, starts off at a tremendous pace, and probably at far too high a pitch. Presently he finds this out by producing a squeak for a high note. But a change of key in the middle of a verse is nothing to him, and he does it without blenching. This is far more courageous than community singing.

Old King Cole also, with innumerable verses, some of which might even have shocked his 'fiddlers three', was a most successful effort. Often the singer has a remarkably fine voice, tenors seem to predominate amongst the country folk of Norfolk - and I had some excellent male voices in the church choir at Brancaster and in a little choral society we had there - though 'nerves' are awkward things to fight against.

VILLAGE FETES

Some of the old village fetes (pronounced *feets* as a rule, much as *cafe* is pronounced so as to rhyme with *safe)* were very amusing. I remember a certain fat piglet that had to be caught by its tail, which was very well greased. The competitors were all the women in the parish over a certain age, and there was a large muster. The pig dashed about all over the place, and the women screamed and fell over each other. Howls of joy were heard whenever a woman succeeded in grasping its tail, only to see that slippery appendage slide through her fingers. Eventually, I regret to say, a very fat old woman fell on the piglet and put it completely out of action. She claimed, and was eventually awarded, the unfortunate animal, but I always considered this a very gross injustice.

Another priceless sight was the male competition of 'Grinning through the horse-collar'. The prize was awarded to the man who could contort his features so appallingly that he could claim to be the ugliest competitor. In this connection I well remember an old countryman who really was extraordinarily ugly. Whether nature had stamped his face or whether a horse had stamped on it, I never knew. He seized the horse collar and was preparing to make a 'face' through it when he was stopped by his friends amid cries of 'Doant yew make no alterations Billa, an yew'll win! Yew'll du as yew are'. This was rude but true, and Billa won handsomely!

COUNTRY SPORTS AND OTHER THINGS

From what I can make out there does not seem to be so much village cricket as there used to be in my young days. I doubt also whether the 'sneak' or 'underhand' bowler is allowed to pursue his devilish machinations quite as freely. In the old days cricket in the villages was most exciting. Given a pitch with several bumps at various intervals - generally laid out between furrows subsequently laid down to grass - an 'equalizing' effect was obtained. The county player was just as likely - generally more likely - to secure a 'duck'.

The village cricketer knew more of the geography, so to speak, of the pitch, whereas the skilled bat, in playing forward stylishly, found that the ball had gone either over or under his bat with surprising quickness - and a very thoughtful man returned to the shelter of the trees to complain bitterly of that 'confounded ploughed field'. On the other hand the cunning villager waited, with his bat very near the ground and almost against the stumps, and seldom ventured to do anything but 'jam on to' a straight ball.

I hope the following story will not be considered vulgar. One Easter an old friend of mine was playing golf at Brancaster, when he had the misfortune to kill a linnet with his ball. He thought this so remarkable that he told his caddie to pocket the poor bird and to give it to him at the end of the game, as he thought he would have it 'set up'.

He forgot all about it and went back to London. Coming down the summer following he happened to have the same caddie, of whom he inquired, 'Do you remember that bird?'

'I reckon I dew an' all' said the man. 'About a week arter you went my old woman she say to me, "Jimma," she say, "yew dew stink suffin awful," she say, an' I sarched and found that ol' bud had gone and slipped trew a hoole in the lining of my pockut. That didn't half stink neither!'

THOUGHTS FROM ABROAD

I heard of two Norfolk men who met in a tavern in the backwoods of Tasmania and were talking somewhat wistfully together of the Old Country. One of them had quoted, rather grandiloquently, Cowper's

England with all thy faults I love thee still

when a voice from the back interjected, 'Ah dessay, an' old Norwich will be all right when they ha' widened Brigg Street!'

DON'T YEW FORGET STOWMARKET

One of Mr. Russell Colman's best stories relates to an elderly gentleman of the countryside who appeared at Trowse Station and waited for the up train to London. The old fellow was somewhat doddering, and was being skilfully shepherded into the train by several female relatives including his 'owd woman'. After considerable 'flusteration' a seat was found for him, but his wife refused to leave the carriage door in spite of the guard's ever-increasing impatience.

'Ha' y' got yer ticket, George?' After much mumbling and searching George found it.

'Ha' y' got yer spittacles?' ... 'Ha' y' got yer hankerchief?' and the like, and, at last, 'Now, George, doan't yew forget, - *Stowmarket !*'

'I know, I know,' said George, 'Stowmarket!'.

At last the train moved off. When they reached Swainsthorpe George put his head out of the window and asked where he was. He repeated the performance when they stopped at Flordon. At Forncett George put his head out again.

'Guard,' he asked, 'is this here Stowmarket ?'

The guard was a bit nettled. 'Set you down you old fule, and I'll tell yew when thas Stowmarket,' and the old man subsided. Diss passed and

Stowmarket came and went before the guard remembered George. Then suddenly, on went the Westinghouse brake and the train was slowly backed into the station again. The guard, by this time, was full of wrath, and went to George, shouting,

'Come out of that now, this here's Stowmarket !' But the old man clung to the carriage.

'I doan't want to get out hare,' he whimpered.

'What do yew mean?' questioned the guard. 'What ha' yew been a bothering me all along about Stowmarket for if yew don't want to get out here ?'

'Well, guard,' said George, 'thass like this hare, afore I left home my old woman she gan me a pill, and she say to me, she say, " Now then, George, *dew yew take another o' them there pills when yew get to Stowmarket"!*'

IVERY TIME YEW YOW

Another story told by Mr. Colman is that during harvest on a certain farm it became necessary that the driver of the cutter should go on working all through the dinner hour to get on with the job. This very naturally amused his mates hugely, and they did their best to 'rub it in'. They all sat at one corner of the barley field, and every time the unfortunate Billa came opposite to them they waved hunks of bread and cheese and mugs of beer, and shouted at him, till he ground his teeth with rage. Finally he stopped opposite to them and said, 'Well, ivery time yew yow, yew lose a chow' and went on.

HOW MANY SHEEP

A certain well-known suffragan bishop was spending his holiday in Norfolk. Being in mufti he travelled in a third-class carriage and happened across an aged man with whom he got into conversation. The bishop asked him how he earned his living.

'I'm a shuppard, maaster,' said the ancient.

'And how many sheep have you in your flock?' inquired the bishop.

'Nigh on t'ree hundred,' replied the shepherd.

The bishop then said, 'It may surprise you, but I, also, am a shepherd. And I have nearly twelve thousand in *my* flock.'

'My heart alive, maaster' was the reply, 'yew must be *main busy in the lambin' season!'*

FIRST TH' OULD SOW DIED

In Norfolk it is unusual for a farm hand to 'live in' with his master, though this is, of course, usual in the 'grass counties'. There was, however one who did so live, for many years, near North Walsham. One day he came to his master and gave notice to leave, and after some inquiry he acknowledged that a neighbouring farmer had 'ticed him away with an offer of another shilling or so per week.

'Well, John, I ain't one to stand in your way' said his master; so off John went. After a month or two John returned and begged to be taken on again.

'Well,' said his old master, 'I ain't suited in your place, but why are you a-leavin' Mr So and So? Doan't they feed ye well?'

'Why, maaster, thass like this hare,' said old John: 't'ree week agoo th' ould sow died, an' we ate har ; last week th' ould cow died, an' we ate har, *an now th' ould missus is dead !'*

DISTRUST AND CURIOSITY

which way did you come? (see page 45)

The Norfolk man has a certain distrust and shows a certain reserve with respect to all *foreigners* - those who have not had the inestimable privilege of being born in his own county. When they come and settle here he treats them with cold civility, is quite prepared to take their money (honestly, of course, and in the way of business), but he eyes them somewhat stealthily, and it is a very long time before he admits them to his closer confidence. All Norfolk men are intensely curious and

43

inquisitive, and are much averse to the giving of any information without receiving a suitable return.

My brother had a friend who was a great 'character'. He was a small man, with a squeaky voice, who had made a lot of money in the old days out of farming and stock-dealing. He was born somewhere on the boundary of Norfolk and Suffolk, but he always pretended to be Suffolk, and criticized the Norfolk folk somewhat severely. He said to my brother one day,

'You Norfolk folk, Mr. Wilson, you are so suspicious. Now you know I still do a bit of farmin' and dealin', tho' o' course, Mr. Wilson, as you know' - with a conscious smirk – 'there ain't no need, for when I go out there's twenty thousand pounds under this old hat o' mine. Well, Mr. Wilson, the other day I'd been over to Bury Market, and I'd had a long day. I wanted to come home when that was very late indeed, an' that was very foggy. (It very often is on market days!) An' when I come in my little old mooter to Winfarthin' well, there I lorst my way!

Now, Mr. Wilson, you know how all them there roads near Winfarthin' go a criss-crossin' about! Well, I druv round and round, and the fog, that fare to git wuss. At last I see a little old cottage on the roadside, and I went and hammered on the door. Arter a wery long time some one lit a candle up in one of them little old bedrooms in the roof like, and a funny little old feller put his hid out of the winder.

"Hello!" says he.

"Hello, yerself !" says I, and I told him I was sorry to distarb him at that time o' night, but I'd lost my way and wanted to get to Wymondham.

"Oh," he say, " Wymondham ?"

"Yis," I say "Wymondham."

"Ah," say he, "now, which way did you come ?"

"Well," I say, "now that doan't matter which way I come, do it ?" I say.

"Noo," he say. "Well, which way *did* you come ?"

Well, then, Mr. Wilson, I lost my temper, I did, and I say to him, I say, "What the devil do it matter to you which way I come ?" I say. "You put me on my way to Wymondham, and I can git on and you can git back to bed !"

And then he say "Noo, that doan't matter to me which way *you come,* and that doan't matter to me which way you *goo*. Good night!" And, Mr. Wilson, he put his hid in and shet the winder!'

Curiously enough, about a week after he heard this story, my brother went over, with his son, to see a house in the Winfarthing district. They got into the right parish, but could not find the house. Eventually they met a labouring man coming along. My brother stopped him and asked, 'Can you tell me where Highfield is ?'

'Highfield ?' said the man in deep thought.

'Now,' he said, *'which way did you come ?'*

*that doan't matter to me which way you come an' that doan't matter which way you goo (*see opposite)

My father was one of a small family of thirteen brothers and one sister! One of his brothers was christened Coombe. He went abroad to Canada when young, and some years afterwards returned on a visit to his native village, Kirby Cane. He was walking round one morning, when he met an old farmer of the parish, whom he used to know. On greeting him, however, it was evident that the farmer did not recognize Coombe.

'Don't you remember me, Mr. G….?' said my uncle.'I'm Coombe'

'Aye,' was the reply, 'I see ye're coom, but now yew are coom, what are yew coom for?'

HE JUST GUESSED IT

A good story is told by a Norwich friend of mine, who asserts that many years back he was driving with a friend of his, their objective being Cromer. His friend was driving, and in trying some short cuts they got lost. However, presently they saw a man ploughing in a field hard by, and the driver shouted to him,

'Hey, Jimma, my lad, which is the way to Cromer ?' The man slowly left his plough, and still more slowly strolled across to them.

'How did yew know,' he asked, with a glint of fury in his eye, 'that my name was Jimma ?'

'Ah' the driver said airily, 'I just guessed it, my lad.'

'Wery well, then,' replied the ploughman, 'yew kin just goo and guess the way to Croomer !' and he returned to his plough.

MY OWD MARE

Two farmers met in the Corn Hall at Norwich one Saturday, and one said, 'Billa, yew look rarely down on yer luck, what is it ?'

'Well, thass my owd mare, George, she fare rarely bad, she dew.'

'Whass wrong wi' her, Billa ?'

Billa explained the mare's complaint, and George said, 'Ah, well now, Billa, my owd hoss, he had the same trouble, and I give him a ball,' and he mentioned a particular and powerful vetinary pill or 'horse ball'.

'Thank ye, George, thank ye kindly' said Billa, and he bustled off in spite of George's effort to stop him. During the following week they met again, and George said, 'Well, Billa, how's the owd mare?'

'Well,' said Billa, 'I gave her that there owd ball, and she's dead!'

'Ah !' said George, 'I meant to tell yew last week, Billa, that my owd hoss, he died too!'

I'LL HAPPEN ACROSS HIM

My father-in-law heard that an old man in his village was going to London to see his son, and asked him where he lived.

'Bethnal Green,' said the old man.

'Oh !' said my father-in-law, 'do you know his exact address ?'

'Noo, I doan't,' replied the ancient, 'but I'll happen across him *somewhere on the Green, noo doubt !'*

THE BAND OF HOPE

Let no one think that our country folk are not very smart with their repartees and rejoinders. As an instance of this I overheard a very smart thing said. A certain *great lady* in our neighbourhood was (very properly) extremely interested in Band of Hope matters, and conceived it her duty to hold a temperance meeting in a barn in an adjoining parish. I was very young at the time, but even a temperance meeting was an 'entertainment' of sorts, so, of course, I went. The lecturer, from the London head-quarters, was a fiery-looking gentleman with a long, grey beard, and he waged exceedingly wroth with us all for what he described as our 'filthy habits!' He went on :

'Why, even the beasts of the field, the beasts of the field, I say, would scorn to indulge in such habits, as you do. For instance,' he said, 'take a donkey. Tie him up alongside a stream of port wine. Would he drink it?' and he glared at us triumphantly. There was a voice came from the back of the barn.

' Tak' yew and tie yew to a hay-stack, maaster, would yew eat that?'

BY THE SEASIDE

There is the story of the Norfolk labourer who was taken by a friend to see the sea. It was his first visit, and his friend, looking north, informed him that it stretched away for hundreds of miles, probably as far as the North Pole.

'Ah dessay !' said the labourer (that word always expresses incredulity). There was only the smoke of a steamer, low down on the horizon, to be seen. The same night at his home pub the labourer was telling a friend what he had seen, and he was more outspoken.

'I know thass a lie,' he said, 'for I seen 'em *a-troshin'* on the other bank!'

THE HARMONIUM

I consider this story to be the best one I have ever heard. Perhaps the story of the peas and the workhouse inmate runs it very close, but that is not printable. Likewise there is the story of the parson who was looking round a strange church and said to the parish clerk, ' I thought there was a reredos here.' The clerk did not exactly know what was meant and merely stated, in a confidential whisper, that, in an emergency, the 'raverend' had a *certain arrangement* in the vestry.

There's a dale o' music in there if yew could but get it out

My father was paying a visit to a couple of old people in our village when he noticed an old harmonium in the corner of the sitting-room.
'I see you have a harmonium there, Mr Tubby,' he said. 'Does any one ever play on it ?'
'Noo, sir, noo,' said old Tubby. 'Noo one doan't never, as ye might say, *play* on it; but yew know, sir, *there's a dale o' music in there if yew could but get it out!'*

THE CONFARMEERTION

The late Bishop of Thetford used to love to tell the story of the Bishop who had held a confirmation in a village in Norfolk and had stayed overnight with the rector. Next day, on going down the street, he came upon some small urchins making mud-pies. The Bishop noticed a quantity of small mud hillocks in a row and asked what they were.

'Please, sir, we are playing confarmeertions,' said one of the boys, 'and them's the boys and gals wot got confarmed.'

'I see,' said his Lordship. 'And where is the Bishop?'

'Ah,' said the boy, 'that take a sight o' muck to make a bishop!'

PERFECT OR IMPERATIVE

The late Mr, Howson, Head Master of Gresham's School, Holt, was anxious to eradicate the Norfolk dialect as far as possible. I believe he thought he had succeeded. One day, however, on coming into the classroom he found that tea, which was overdue, was not ready. He turned, with some impatience, issued the following instruction to one of the boys:

'Have that bell rung!'

The boy at once said, 'No, sir, that ha'en't; not yit that ha'en't.'

THE TRAIN

I am taken to task for having omitted that white-whiskered father of all Norfolk stories concerning the labourer and the train. Somewhere about the middle of last century Walter said to Ephraim,

'Ha' yew seen the train, Ephra ?'

'Noo, I ha'en't,' said Ephra.

'Well, if yew goo up top o' yin hill a little better'n half arter fower to-morrrer arternoon yew'll see har,' said Walter.

They met next evening.

'Did yew see the train, Ephra ?' said Walter.

'Yes, that I did an' all. I went up atop o' yin hill, as yew said, Walter, this arternoon, and set me down; presently she come a-puffin' along, owd hotguts did; then, dang me! if she didn't see me all of a sudden-like, and, lawk ! as soon as she spotted me alooking at her she *shruk out* and darted into a gret trench and ran away in a mooment.'

THE SHELDUCK

A Norfolk man likes to wrap up his explanation as much as possible.
Some wonderful simile is sometimes dragged in to point his moral and
adorn his tale. A friend of mine shot a shelduck and asked a marshman
if it were good to eat. The latter would not commit himself so far, but
said, 'Well, sir, yew should take and get an owd brick and put that inter
the oven with yar owd shelduck, and when you kin git a fork inter that
there owd brick yar owd shelduck'll be fit t'eat !'

HARD O' HEARING

A certain youth was busy with others trying to shoot rabbits in a wood.
The poor rabbits ran hither and thither and all the guns were very busy.
The youth, however, had no success whatever. Finally one poor
bemused rabbit sat quite still in a ride within about ten yards of our
friend. He took careful aim and fired, but the beast took no notice. Then
an old 'brusher' said 'Goo on, sir. Hev another goo at 'im. *Happen he
didn't hear ye the fust time'.*

On a bitter day in December a party of guns were not doing very well
with the 'buds'. An ancient 'brusher' sympathized with one of the guns.
He said, 'Bless ye, sir, their owd skins git so haard yew can't get the
shot into 'em!'

Another'brusher' was more critical over the capabilities of the guns.
'Blast me!' he said, 'they wouldn't kill 'em if them cattridges was
loaden with *chain harrers !'*

BIG GAME

And, while on shooting stories, Sir Bartle Frere was much amused with
his keeper, who has a dry sense of humour. There had been a big flush
of pheasants and the guns had been hard at it, with birds flying back
with the wind. After the drive the keeper came back for approbation.

'Very good, indeed; they came very well,' said Sir Bartle. 'It reminds
me of a friend of mine who killed fourteen wild elephants with fifteen
shots!'

The keeper was not unduly impressed. All he said was, *'Hope he'd got
his game-bag with him!'*

BUTTER

A new parson had come to the village. The wife of a small farmer said to her boy, 'Now then, John, when yew ha' got yer tea I want yew to run down to the ractory and take the new raverend half a pound o' my butter. Happen he'll like that, and that may lead to business'

So John duly delivered the butter, and while so engaged the new *raverend* heard the conversation at the hall-door and popped out of his study with a 'What's this? What's this?' John spoke up.

'My ma she sent yer this hare butter, as a prasent like,' upon which the rector said,

'Well, now, that's very kind of her. What beautiful butter. And how does she do all that fancy scrollwork on top of the butter, my lad?'

'Oo that ain't half easy,' said John. *'She do that with our comb'*

THE TEDDY BEAR

A small girl was presented with a Teddy bear whose eyes were set wrong in its head - a little on the 'sosh'! She christened it 'Gladly'. On her mother asking for the reason, she said, 'It's after the hymn, Mother.' 'What do you mean, dear?' said her mother.

'Why, you know, Mother, at Sunday School we sing " gladly *my cross-eyed bear"!'*

JOURNEYS

I can hardly believe the story of the old woman who decided to join her son in Australia. On a friend sympathizing with her over the length of the journey, she is supposed to have said,

'Well, ye see, that 'oon't be so bad. I'm a'goin' to break the jarney at Wymondham'.

SPLENDID ISOLATION

A relation of mine was talking to an old gardener of his and mentioned Hemblington Pond (which pond is situated about two miles from the old man's house). To the surprise of my relation the old man didn't know of it.

'Ye see, sir', he said, 'I doan't *go about a sight !'*

Canon Marcon tells me that he had an old parishioner, one Philip. The Canon met him one day walking towards Briston with another old man who was a stranger to the Canon. On being subsequently asked who he was walking with, Philip replied 'My brother,' and then gave Canon M. the whole 'pedigree' of their meeting.

'I was a-standin',' he said, 'a-leanin' over my gate when an owd man came up and spoke to me. Who he was I didn't know.

"Philip" he say, "I'm a-comin' in hare" - and so he did. And when he clapped me on the back, clare to me if that worn't my brother George'.

'Of course,' said the Canon, 'I suppose you hadn't seen him for a long time'

'Not for saveral years,' said old Philip; 'he'd abin away'

The Canon's mind wandered to Kamschatka or Australia, and he asked 'Where had he been to?'

'Briston', (which was the next parish).

The Canon was so surprised that he couldn't help laughing, which apparently offended old Philip.

'Oh, no! he hadn't been at Briston all the time.' explained Philip.

'Where had he been then?' asked the Canon.

'Hunworth o'course' (another adjoining parish). Neither of the parishes was more than two miles from Edgefield!

HIS HOBBY

A man I know was wandering about in a churchyard in a remote part of the county when he saw a man (the parish clerk as it turned out) digging a grave in a corner. He asked the man who was dead, and the old fellow replied,

'Thass the wife of our raverend - and thass his thud wife, an all. And' (in a hoarse, confidential whisper) 'he moostly bury 'em in this hare corner - thass his *hobby !*'

,

POOR OLD BILLA

A farmer's son came in one day and said to his father,

' Owd Billa ha' hung hisself in the barn.'

'Lawk !' said his father. 'Did yew cut 'im down? '

'Noo, that I din't.'

'Why not ?'

'cos *he wrorn't dead*'

Thass his hobby (see opposite)

WIVES

Two old Norfolk men met. Said one to the other, 'Hello! Billa, yew look rarely down in the mouth. Whass the matter wi' ye? '

' Nothin' much Tom,' the other replied.

'Oh! Where a yew a-goin'?' Tom asked.

'I'm a-goin' up to see the doctor.'

'What for?' Tom demanded.

'Well, I doan't like the look o' my missis.' Said Billa.

'Well, blow me if I doan't come along wi' ye,' said Tom. 'I *haate the sight o' mine!*'

THEM BEWTIFUL BELLS

Two old fellows stood in Norwich Market Place. St. Peter Mancroft's bells were in full swing. One of the old men was very deaf indeed. The other said to him, 'Kin yew hare them bewtiful bells ?'

'Hey ?' said the other.

Same question, only louder.

'Wass that yew say? I can't hare ye.'

The other bellowed in his ear, 'I say, kin yew hare them bewtiful bells?' And then the reply came,

'I can't hare *wot* yew say, these hare owd bells make such a din!'

A FINE WOMAN

A Norwich friend of mine has an uncle who is a farmer in a certain village in Norfolk. His uncle is a very small man, but his aunt weighs sixteen stone or so. My friend was staying with them, and one morning at breakfast his aunt stated that she had an 'itch' in her back and asked her nephew if he would kindly scratch it for her. He at once complied, but in spite of her directions he could not locate the exact spot. Finally her husband said

'Lave har alone, John; the wumman doan't know *to an acre* where she dew itch!'

EQUINOCTIAL GALES

There was a brisk business-like widow in our parish with whom my father very frequently had a 'mardle' when on his village rounds. On one occasion - somewhere about Lady Day - during a blustering wind, my father stopped by Mrs. B's gate to pass the time of day. The countryside was at the time very much preoccupied with all the auction sales advertised on the various farms.

'Morning, Mrs. B,' said my father. 'Very blustering, isn't it ?   I suppose we must expect this now, owing to the equinoctial gales, of course.'

Mrs. B didn't quite catch the reference, but replied readily,

'Well, now you mention it, sir, I hev noticed that the wind is very strong *the week of the* auction *sales!'*

AMATEUR'S EXPENSES

It has always been a vexed question as to how far an amateur should be paid expenses when playing for his country or his county. It is now generally agreed that he should be paid all reasonable expenses. In the old days when the Norfolk cricket team played an out match we were allowed enough to cover rail fares and hotel expenses. This meant, as a rule, a grant of from two to three pounds per match. When that best and most generous of men, the late Mr. E. G. Buxton, was honorary treasurer, he was so honorary that it must have cost him a great deal of money. He was the great 'maker up of deficits'. I doubt if his like will ever be seen in Norfolk again, and the gap he left can never quite be filled.

On one occasion, a few days after a match at Cambridge, one of the most enterprising of our young players - whom I will call Sparrow - called in at the bank.

'Morning, Sparrow' said E. G. 'What can I do for you?' Sparrow cleared his throat.

'It's- er - about my expenses to Cambridge, Mr. Buxton,' he said.

'Oh, yes, of course, Sparrow. Let me see. How much do you want?' Sparrow gently mentioned the sum of *seven* pounds or so.

'Heavens! Sparrow, you can't have spent all that,' said E. G.

' Oh, but, Mr. Buxton,' said Sparrow naively, *'you should just have seen the cards I held in the train!'*

E. G. was so amused that, I am told, he paid up in full. He was that sort of man.

RURAL SOCIALISM

Two smallholders attended their first Socialist meeting in the village. On the way home one said to the other, 'Well, now, George, is that right what he say?'

'I reckon that fare to be. Thass like this hare. If yew had two hosses, Jimma, and I dint hev any, yew'd gi' me one on em', woont yew? '

'Ah! I would an' all, George.'

'An' if *I* had two cows, and *yew* dint hev any, *I'd* be sure to gi' *yew* one on 'em woont I ?'

'Yes, George, sartainly yew would.'

'An' if yew had saveral pigs – '

' Ooh aah, yew duzzy owd fule, George !   *Yew know I keep pigs!*'

THE MOLE-CATCHER

A certain Canon, in a south Norfolk town, was anxious to induce the local 'moll'-catcher to come to church. He tried him with three or four roundabout questions, to all of which the old man returned 'fencing' replies. Eventually the Canon said,

'I am sorry to say I have not worshipped in the same building with you lately, Sam.' The old man gave the Canon an 'old-fashioned' look, and said,
'Doan't yew know, sir, as yew should never set a trap for the same moll in the *same* place *twice!*'

AVIATION

Many, many years ago an old lady at Dennington very strongly objected to aeronautical balloons when they were first invented. She said, 'That dew fare so *bumptious* to the Almighty!'

SUNDAY SCHOOL

A small boy was asked, 'Why did Joseph tell his brethren not to fall out by the way?' And his answer was, 'Please, ma'am, there worn't no tailpiece to the caart!'

THREE PARSONS

'Yes, I ha' seen a dale o' change in this hare parish, and I ha' sarved under saveral parsons,' said the old clerk - 'tree on 'em. The fust raverend were one of them owd butterfly catchers; he thowt o' nothin' but butterflies an' moths, and he an' the next one was both on 'em jolly sort of men. He used to call me the parish *beetle.* The next one he was a naval man, he was, and he called me the *sextant,* he did. And this hare one we ha' got now he's wot they call, I think, one of them Angular Catholics, and he ha' dressed me up in a black gown and he call me the vargin.'

MATTINS

'Let me see,' said a visitor to the old parish clerk. ' Do you have matins now in this church? '
'Noo, sir, noo, not now we doan't. But we dew hev linoleum right up the whole way as far as the altar! '

MARE AND FOAL SONG

I remember being very much pleased with an ancient song sung at merry-makings at Fritton long ago. It appears from the song that a mare and foal one summer afternoon wander into the churchyard and finding the church doors open the mare climbs into the pulpit while the foal takes the parish clerk's desk. The mare then proceeds to criticize all the local worthies in rhyme, and at the end of each verse the foal says, 'Amen'. The squire, the parson, the doctor all come under review. I am sorry to say I can only remember a few lines, and even those, I fear, imperfectly :

thus said *The Mare :*

God rest the good carrier what goes on the road,
And give him good going to lighten his load,
And if he should happen t'get inter a hole
I wish 'um seft out.   *"Amen"said the foal.*

And 'seft' for 'saved', or 'safe', is another beautiful Norfolk word.

THE 'WOTE'

This story concerns two Conservatives and one Labour supporter.

The Labour man received his instructional *pro forma* ballot paper and couldn't make head nor tail of it. He was unwise enough to consult his Conservative friends. 'Doan't yew see, William, what yew ha' got to dew?'

 William didn't.

'Well, yew ha' just got to put a cross agin that one what yew *doan't* want to get in - yew cross *him* off right clare, ye see'; and I am afraid the Conservative candidate was two up on balance.

THE PHENOMENOM

During a bout of *very* wet weather the barometers (for some reason known only to themselves) persistently registered 'Set fine'. An irate old farmer, anxious to get on with his haysel, was heard to say,

 'I fared right tired of the mucky owd thing; so I takes th' owd *phenomenon* and I lays him on the path in the garden, an' I ses, " Thare," I ses, " yew kin see for yourself whether that rain or no !" '

Another old farmer smashed his barometer to pieces with a stick because it didn't tell the truth.

THE PRACTICAL PARTNER

 I am afraid the following is rather an old story - I remember that it amused my father considerably. An impoverished Norfolk parson was

Yew kin see for yourself whether that rain or no (see opposite)

suddenly and most unexpectedly offered rather a fat living. On hearing this a friend hurried to the rectory to offer his congratulations. The parson's daughter came to the door. 'I've called to see your father,' said the friend.

'Very sorry, he's engaged,' said the daughter.

'Very well then, I'll see your mother.'
'Afraid you can't. She's engaged too'
'Good gracious me!' said the friend. 'What on earth are they both doing?'
'Well, Father is in his study *praying for guidance,* and *Mother's a packing!'*

THE WONDERS OF STEAM

The oldest inhabitant at Brancaster used to stand at the marsh gates all day and earn a pittance by opening them occasionally. The wife of one of the members of the golf-club stopped one day and had a mardle with him. An aeroplane was flying overhead. 'How would you like to be up in that Mr. G,' she said.
'Noo ma'am, I doan't think I want to go a-flyin',' he said; 'but thass a wonder what *stame* will dew in these hare days.'

TRICOLATION

My gardener and I were pondering over the possible rejuvenation of an old mowing-machine. Eventually he shook his head despondently and said
'Happen I could *tricolate* that up a bit, but that 'oon't be a sight o' good, I doubt.'
Also of some newly-laid turf he said, 'Thass a-drawin' together nicely but thass *new time* yet'

THE SCYTHE

This is a queer beast and very few amateurs can use it. Many years ago, on a summer evening, my mother called my father's attention to the state of our lawn at Fritton. We had a very long-serving gardener in those days and he was very set in his ways, performing his various tasks as and when *he* thought fit. The grass had got too long for the mowing-machine. My father assumed a firm, determined look and said, 'Very well, my dear, I'll teach Marshall a lesson. Example is better than precept!'
So next morning we all woke to the sound of the scraping of the hone on the blade, and were exhilarated by the sight of my father, stripped for

action, on the lawn. It was a hot morning. Some time after eight Marshall rolled up. My father ceased for a moment, mopped the honest sweat from his brow, and said, 'There, Marshall, you see what can be done if one gets up early' - and waited for applause.

Old Marshall gave one sour look at my father, another at the lawn, which was a shambles of tussocks and 'divots', and replied, *'Well, sir, I reckon yew'd ha' bin better a-bed !'*

PARTNERSHIP

The ingenuous nature of some of our country folk is very extraordinary. Years ago when whist was a very popular country game, a friend of mine noticed that his coachman and the gardener would always play as partners together if possible. He remarked on this and said to coachman, 'Walker, why is it that you and Thompson always want to play together and never seem happy when we part you?' Walker naively replied, 'Well y' see, sir, me and Thompson we understands one another's play so well. He allus keep his foot agin mine, and one tap mean play the ace and two taps mean play the king and so on, y' see.'

he allus keep his foot agin mine

POETIC LICENCE

Many years ago there was an outbreak of sheep stealing in Norfolk. One old farmer had been particularly unfortunate, so he has some bills printed offering a reward of ten pounds for information that would lead to a conviction and duly posted a copy on the side of his barn.

The next morning another sheep had gone and written under his notice were the following lines: -

You are rich and we are poor.
Your mutton's good – we'll ha' some more!

CANINE LITERACY

Two old Norfolk farmers were coming past Costessey Park. For some reason the owner, Lord Stafford, had been troubled by poachers and had posted notices at various places saying '*Traps have been set for Dogs*'. One of the old fellows slowly read the notice and then turned to his companion and said 'Yis! Thass all wery well, but there aint one damn dawg in a thousand what can read it!'

THE ALTERNATIVE

Of course I am a poacher. Mr Russell Colman is a magistrate, but I must risk a conviction in a good cause. And this is a good one which he told me. A civil assize action was being heard at Norwich, I am told, and one of the plaintiff's witnesses was a country lad, son of the plaintiff, who was a farmer in a small way. The lad was not too bright and the judge wished to make quite sure that he understood the nature of an oath and the real difference between truth and perjury; so his Lordship said,

'Now tell me, my lad, did your father tell you what would happen to you if you swore falsely in the witness-box?'

'Yus, he did an' all,' said the boy; 'he said I'd *go to hell!*'

'Very likely, very likely,' said the judge; 'and did he say what would happen if you spoke the truth?

'That he did' said the boy; ' *he said we'd lose the Bl--dy action!*'

Now tell me, my lad, did your father tell you what would happen to you if you swore falsely in the witness-box (see opposite)

THE SWEEPSTAKE

A Brundall gentleman, on a whim, presented his old gardener with a ticket in the Irish Grand National Sweepstake and the promoters presented him with a blank. His master, sympathizing with him, remarked that he could hardly expect to draw a horse. The old man however was not satisfied and remained very suspicious.

'Ah dessay' he said; 'but that fare mighty quare to me that *nobody in Brundall ha'ent drawn none nayther.'*

Broad Norfolk
By Jonathan Mardle

If you enjoyed reading *Norfolk Tales,* you're sure to love *Broad Norfolk* by Jonathan Mardle – one of Norfolk's best-loved writers.

Jonathan Mardle was the pseudonym of Eric Fowler well-known author, essayist and leader writer of the **Eastern Daily Press** *with which he was associated for over fifty years*

Recently voted one of the ten greatest books ever written about the county, **Broad Norfolk** *is illustrated by the late Joe Lee - one of Britain's foremost cartoonists who, after 32 years on the* **Evening Standard** *in London retired to Norwich where he continued to contribute cartoons to the* **E.D.P***.*

Described as "one of the most important contributions ever made to Norfolk dialect" **Broad Norfolk** *is as fresh and entertaining now as when it first became a classic best-seller.*

Broad Norfolk by Jonathan Mardle

Illustrated by Lee

Published by Prospect Press at £5.95